Contents

Introduction　　　　　　　　　　　　　　　2
Sir David Attenborough

Kew: a short history　　　　　　　　　　　3

1 In search of plants　　　　　　　　　　4

2 The gardens: science and beauty　　　8

3 Understanding the plant kingdom　　14

4 Saving plants from extinction　　　　22

5 Spreading the word　　　　　　　　　28

6 The future　　　　　　　　　　　　　32
Ghillean T. Prance
Director, Royal Botanic Gardens, Kew

Resources　　　　　　　　　　　　　　　34

Introduction

Sir David Attenborough

The tradition of excellence in botanical research at Kew is long-standing and dates back to the nineteenth century and its first director, Sir William Hooker, who began the study of plants that could be useful to humanity – a discipline known as 'economic botany'. Kew's early involvement in the development of rubber and quinine is well known, as is its role in the transporting of breadfruit from Tahiti to the West Indies – a project that led to the mutiny on the *Bounty*. Less well known are the early studies on plant cellulose, which eventually resulted in the viscose-rayon and acetate fibre industry. This tradition continues today with vital research on cures for AIDS, on plant sources of insect 'anti-feedants' as potentially 'safe' insecticides, and on the development of new programmes in molecular biology – all are at the heart of Kew's activities.

Behind all of these are the plants themselves. Kew continues to send out expeditions to every part of the world to collect material for study and eventually to introduce new species to cultivation. The seed-collecting programme is rapidly expanding to add more species to what is already the most significant collection on earth: the World Seed Bank at Wakehurst Place, Kew's annexe in West Sussex.

Kew's work now has a new urgency as changes to and destruction of the earth's natural habitats and the plants they contain increase – with far-reaching consequences for the future of life on earth. Kew's botanists and horticulturists are able to help solve global problems by advising on environmental management, preserving endangered species – both as seeds and as living plants – and searching for alternative crops as sources of food, fuel and medicine.

As a trustee of the Royal Botanic Gardens, Kew, I am delighted to have the opportunity to introduce a publication that affords a glimpse behind the beautiful public face of the Gardens to their other vital roles of scientific research and education.

David Attenborough

Kew: a short history

1759, Augusta, Dowager Princess of Wales and mother of George III, began a botanic garden of about 9 acres (3.5 ha) her estate at Kew. Sir William Chambers designed a number buildings for her, including the Orangery, Pagoda and ined Arch.

Sir Joseph Banks, who was an enthusiastic plant collector as a young man, organised Kew's first plant hunting expeditions

1772, George III had inherited both the Kew property and e neighbouring Richmond estate, which ran along the ames between Richmond and Kew, and the two were entually joined together. During the king's reign, Sir Joseph nks was the unofficial director of the botanic garden, and nt out an army of young men into the world to bring back ants to Kew. Both Banks and the king died in 1820, and the rden went into a temporary decline.

1840, the botanic garden was handed over to the state and, ortly afterwards, was enhanced by a gift of land from the yal family which increased it to over 200 acres (81 ha). The lowing year, Sir William Hooker was appointed the first ficial director, and during his time at Kew, the Palm House d the Temperate House were completed and the Economic tany Museums, the Herbarium and the Library were

established. Public enthusiasm for Kew also increased: the annual number of visitors grew from 9000 in 1841 to half a million in 1865, the year of Sir William's death.

He was succeeded by his son Joseph Hooker (later Sir Joseph), who was already well known as a plant-hunter, having sailed to Antarctica, New Zealand and Tasmania (1839-43) and traversed the slopes of Nepal and Sikkim (1847-51). His principal contribution to Kew was establishing it as a centre of experimental scientific research by founding the Jodrell Laboratory in 1876. After his retirement in 1885, the Gardens were expanded and enhanced by his successors, until, today, they comprise slightly more than 300 acres (121 ha), and are visited by well over one million people every year.

In 1965, the Royal Botanic Gardens took over Wakehurst Place in West Sussex. This estate of 499 acres (202 ha), with its rich collection of mature trees and Southern Hemisphere plants, is leased from the National Trust for a peppercorn rent. Part of the woodland on the estate has been designated a 'Site of Special Scientific Interest', and the Loder Valley Reserve includes three major habitat types and provides protection for the endangered plants of the Sussex Weald.

This cycad, Encephalartos altensteinii, is the oldest glasshouse plant in the world; it was sent to Kew from South Africa in 1775

The maidenhair tree, Ginkgo biloba, close to the Orangery was planted in Princess Augusta's botanic garden in 1761

1

In search of plants

Even in this age of satellite mapping and mass tourism, there are still many parts of the world that have not been explored botanically. The careful collection of plants from the wild has always been an integral part of the work of the Royal Botanic Gardens at Kew – and in fact, almost every Kew plant-hunting expedition discovers species new to science.

When Kew sends out an expedition – and it always does so in partnership with scientists of the host country – its aims are to discover and bring into cultivation plants and seeds for horticultural and scientific study; to gather other plant material for identification; and to document as much information as possible about each plant and its location, surroundings and uses. This kind of carefully organised and scientifically controlled plant collecting does not conflict with the aims of conservation. Indeed, detailed collecting and later analysis gives conservationists much-needed information about which species grow in a given area, what their value to humanity is, whether particular species are rare and what conservation action needs to be taken.

Conservation v. exploitation

In recent years, with the world's plants disappearing at a terrifyingly accelerated rate – especially in the tropical and subtropical forests, and mainly through loss of habitat – it has become vital to explore these regions and bring into cultivation the rarer and scientifically more interesting species, some of which are, potentially, enormously valuable.

The numbers of samples collected during expeditions are very small relative to the vegetation of an area. In fact, these numbers are infinitesimal in comparison to the wholesale exploitation by commercial logging companies and, in some cases, by unscrupulous traders in particular groups of plants, such as cacti, bulbous plants and orchids – many species are thought to have been brought to the verge of extinction in this way. Collecting living examples of rare and endangered species enables scientists at Kew and elsewhere to study them in cultivation, and when the plants have become established, they can act as a reservoir to reinforce wild populations so that these do not become extinct. And it is only by scientific study that the potential of these species as edible, medicinal or decorative plants can be assessed.

In many parts of the world, the plants making up the characteristic vegetation have never been studied in any depth. It is essential to compile full catalogues –

Sir Joseph Hooker (seated on left) on a collecting expedition in Colorado, 1877

This logging camp in Nabawan, Sabah, covers the last known site of a species of orchid, Corybas piliferus

lled *Floras* – and checklists of the pecies present now, so that we can onitor the effects that we have on our nvironment and assess the ecological mportance of each region. In the past, ew has been involved in the production Floras for Africa, Australia, India, prus and Iraq, and there is continuing rk on those for west tropical, east and uth-central Africa. Today, new studies ve been concentrating on regions here the vegetation is particularly verse, or of special concern for the nservation of genetic resources. unei (on the north coast of Borneo in e South China Sea) and Brazil are ime examples.

ilful tree climbers can collect mples of leaves, stems and flowers thout damaging the tree

Out in the field

Wild plant material is gathered in a number of different ways. Specimens that will be used for identification are collected when they are in flower; they are dried by being placed between sheets of absorbent paper and squeezed in a plant press, then bundled up and sealed in waterproof containers for shipment. In the tropics, where the climate is very humid, the specimens may be placed in a preservative alcohol solution in plastic bags, to be dried later; this solves the common problem of drying plants being destroyed by moulds. Fruits and seeds are cleaned, carefully dried and then placed in linen bags or paper envelopes. Delicate flowers are often kept in an alcohol-based solution in tubes or jars. Many orchids, cacti and bulbs are simply placed dry in boxes or packets, in which they will keep for weeks.

If possible, plants that will be used for cultivation are collected as seeds, but when this is not possible, seedlings or cuttings are gathered. These must be kept alive during transit back to Kew, and how this is to be done can often tax the ingenuity of even the most experienced plant-hunter. Every plant or piece of plant material sent back to Kew is accompanied by full field notes (*see* Chapter 2).

Each year, Kew sends a number of

expeditions to various parts of the world. These range from short study visits by individuals wishing to look in detail at a particular group of plants – cacti, orchids or palms, for instance – to teams making more general collections. In both cases, the Kew botanists link up with horticulturists and botanists of the host countries, so that all can benefit from the expeditions' work, sharing the teams' knowledge and the plants and data collected.

Specimens are carefully dried and pressed in the field

On the slopes of Kanchenjunga

Dr Christopher Grey-Wilson, expedition leader

The area around Kanchenjunga has a particularly rich and diverse flora

In the late summer of 1989, an expedition organised jointly by the Royal Botanic Gardens, Kew and Royal Botanic Garden, Edinburgh was sent to the Kanchenjunga region of north-eastern Nepal.

Botanically, this is a rich country with a wide range of flora, from the subtropical lowlands of the Terai, to the Himalayan foothills where broad-leaved deciduous and evergreen forests cover the slopes, and on up to higher elevations – to nearly 14,000 ft (4270 m) – dominated by evergreen coniferous forests, together with rhododendrons, birch and a host of different shrubs. Above the tree-line, meadows, rock outcrops, screes, cliffs, moraines and marshes provide a variety of different habitats in which a great many alpine plants are to be found – among them, gentians, saxifrages, primulas and blue poppies **(Meconopsis)**.

Himalayan blue poppy, *Meconopsis horridula*

The region chosen to explore is a particularly interesting one. It has only been re-opened to expeditions in recent years, and having hardly any roads and being a long way from the capital Kathmandu, it is not on one of the usual tourist trails. In addition, this part of Nepal, dominated by the huge

Sketch of Kanchenjunga by Joseph Hooker

massif of Kanchenjunga, the world's third highest mountain, is fairly thinly populated and large areas of fine forest still remain.

Historically, eastern Nepal and the neighbouring kingdom of Sikkim are closely linked to Kew. It was here that, between 1848 and 1850, an expedition was led by Joseph Hooker. An accomplished draughtsman, plant-collector, surveyor and scientist, he was especially interested in the rhododendrons and balsams **(Impatiens)** that grew in profusion in this region, and he wrote copious notes and made numerous illustrations of what he saw – later published in two volumes as **Hooker's Himalayan Journal**.

The 1989 expedition chose to travel in Nepal in late August, September and early October. This period spans the last half of the monsoon season – when there are still many plants in bloom – and early autumn, when the rains usually cease, the weather is briefly mild and sunny before the onset of the Himalayan winter, and it is the best time to collect seeds.

Setting off

In the expedition team were three members each from Kew and Edinburgh, who were variously interested in **Impatiens**, alpine plants, mosses (bryophytes) and Liliaceae and related families, as well as the general vegetation of the area. Since medical facilities were virtually non-existent where we were going, we were also accompanied by a doctor, and as we were working in collaboration with the Department of Forests and Soil Conservation in Kathmandu, we were joined by their Dr Mahendra Subedi, a forest ecologist.

An enormous amount of planning and work goes into mounting an expedition of this type. Budgets need to be carefully calculated; the equipment for collecting and camping must be determined; and personal belongings are assessed to the last detail, right down to how many rolls of film, pairs of socks and ballpoint pens to take. For this expedition, planning in Britain had to be carefully co-ordinated with the Nepalese authorities and with the company organising the trekking side.

The team arrived in Kathmandu at the end of the third week of August. After three days spent finalising arrangements, we set off, the entire expedition now consisting of the British members, Dr Subedi, five Sherpas, two cooks and some 55 porters who were responsible for carrying all the equipment through the mountains. A bus of noble vintage transported us east – with a few delays due to a plethora of punctures and chronic gear problems – to just above the town of Hille, well to the west of Kanchenjunga, where the road became impassable. For the next seven weeks, we walked.

Leeches and swirling mists

We first traversed some high ridges (up to 10,000 ft/3050m), eventually descending to the Tamur river, which we travelled

Porters transported the expedition's equipment and plant collections and set up the campsites

Photo: Christopher Grey-Wilson

along to its junction with the Ghunsa Khola. We followed this valley, reaching up to more than 15,000 ft (4575m) above the summer settlement of Lhonak, where the landscape is dominated by high icy peaks, massive glaciers, cliffs and enormous plunging screes. Unfortunately for us, the weather did not co-operate: most days, it was wet, and often we walked and worked in driving rain and swirling mists. Worst still, we were afflicted with hosts of blood-sucking leeches! As we travelled, the Sherpas and porters had to set up camps, light fires and prepare meals every night; then, the following morning, they had to pack up everything, rain or shine. Our collecting continued, too. We searched out both seeds and specimens, the latter having to be carefully dried and annotated – a time-consuming occupation each evening.

While we were camped in Ghunsa, tragedy struck: the death (apparently from pneumonia) of one of the porters, who had been sent ahead to prepare our visit to an adjacent valley. There was nothing we could do other than follow the official Nepalese procedures in such an event: by the time we had arrived in the next valley, the cremation had already

taken place. It was a reminder to us of the frailty of human life in these remote regions of the world.

We continued on, crossing several high passes, all above 15,000 ft (4575 m), and then descending to Yalung in the Kabeli valley. The lower part of this uninhabited valley contains the most beautiful forests, primarily coniferous but with an understorey of many different species of smaller trees and shrubs, as well as colourful herbaceous plants. The expedition later recommended to the Nepalese authorities that this region should be set aside as an important national park or reserve, not only because of its trees and other plants, but also for the wide range of animal life – mammals, birds, insects and reptiles – found there.

The last ten days of the expedition were spent near the small town of Yamphudin, which Joseph Hooker had visited nearly 140 years before. It was fascinating to compare the details recorded in his journal with what we saw now: the area was very little changed. We had left the wet weather behind, and by the time we returned to Kathmandu, most of the collections had been dried. One set of all we had collected remained in Nepal, for that country's botanists to research.

The end of an expedition is no time to relax. We had to sort out all our specimens, box and despatch them, complete our field notes and diaries, write our reports and balance our budgets. Back in Britain, a second set of what we had collected would be sent on to Edinburgh, and the constituents of a third would be carefully named and incorporated into Kew's Herbarium. The seeds would be sown and cultivated, and those not retained by Kew or Edinburgh would be distributed to other institutes and growers. The dried and live specimens we collected on the slopes of Kanchenjunga will remain as historical data for future analysis by botanists and horticulturists.

Photo: Christopher Grey-Wilson

The expedition's campsite at Ghunsa Khola, south of Lhonak

2

The gardens: science and beauty

Plants arrive at Kew – and at its satellite garden, Wakehurst Place in West Sussex – from all over the world. Sometimes they are sent by other botanical institutes, but more often they arrive back with expeditions sent out by the Royal Botanic Gardens.

The expedition's field notes about a plant in the wild are as important as the specimen collected. Without data on where it was found, the surrounding vegetation, the soil, the climatic conditions and the altitude at which it was growing, staff at Kew will not know how best to treat a newly arrived plant – not to mention the data's use as a vital record for scientific and conservation purposes. Each plant's details are transferred to a computer database maintained at Kew – the **Index Vivendae** *– after the plant has been given a unique ten-figure 'accession' number. This number can be seen on the label displayed with the plant.*

All specimens coming to Kew from abroad are held in a quarantine glasshouse for a time, to make sure that no pests or diseases are accidentally introduced into Britain. Then they are sent to one of the nursery glasshouses, where they will be established and propagated. If a plant is the only one of its kind at Kew – and especially if it is endangered in the wild – it will be held in one of the reserve collections for safe-keeping and, whenever possible, propagated to increase its numbers, prior to distribution to other botanic gardens or reintroduction into the wild. After propagation, plants are sent to one of the five sections that comprise Kew's collection of living plants:

♦ the *Alpine and Herbaceous Section*, including the Alpine House, woodland, aquatic, rock and grass gardens, the 'Herbaceous Ground' and decorative beds such as those in the Duke's Garden, the Palm House Parterre and the seventeenth-century-style Queen's Garden.

♦ the *Arboretum Section* containing trees and shrubs, including the rose garden, the bamboo garden and the rhododendron dell.

♦ the *Temperate Section* responsible for the tender woody plants grown in the Palm and Temperate houses and the Australian and Waterlily houses.

♦ the *Tropical Section*, in which are grown most of the tender herbaceous plants, displayed in the Princess of Wales Conservatory and the Filmy Fern House.

Alternatively, a plant may be sent to *Wakehurst Place*. Species from the wetter parts of the Southern Hemisphere grow better there because the rainfall is considerably greater than at Kew, sheltered sites are available and danger from frost is reduced. Similarly, the moister, cooler conditions there suit temperate Himalayan forest plants such as rhododendrons.

Providing the right conditions

All wild plants have become adapted to survive under the prevailing conditions in their natural habitats, and to grow them successfully at Kew, their natural environment must be reproduced as far as possible.

For instance, there are ten different environment types within the Princess of

Wales conservatory – ranging from arid desert to moist cloud forest – which enables Kew to cultivate plants from all the tropical regions of the world.

Plants from the deserts of Africa and America

Lush vegetation from the hot humid rainforests

Maintaining these environments is not easy: conditions within each one are checked automatically every two minutes to ensure that the humidity, temperature, light and ventilation are correct, and these are adjusted when necessary.

Architecture at Kew and Wakehurst Place

The Royal Botanic Gardens not only maintain collections of many of the world's plants, they are also custodians of a remarkable collection of buildings, of which the following are only the most substantial.

The Pagoda   Designed for Princess Augusta (mother of George III) by Sir William Chambers in 1761-62. Octagonal, ten storeys, 163 ft (50 m) high. Once decorated with 80 glass dragons (sold to pay off George IV's debts). Not open to visitors.

The Palm House   Kew's 'Crystal Palace'. Designed by Decimus Burton with Richard Turner. Constructed 1844-48. Covers 24,200 sq. ft (2248 sq. m).

The Tudor Mansion, Wakehurst Place   Built in 1590 for Edward Culpeper (a relative of the famous herbalist). Substantially altered over the last 400 years but the Tudor façade remains.

Princess of Wales Conservatory   Built 1983-85, to replace 26 smaller houses and sections of houses. Designed to be economic to run and maintain – e.g. much of the interior is below ground to save heat, and the building is orientated to make the best use of light. Now Kew's largest glasshouse, covering 48,332 sq. ft (4490 sq. m).

The Temperate House   Designed by Decimus Burton; constructed 1860-62 (main block and octagons) and 1896-99 (wings), when it became the largest glasshouse in the world, covering 47,912 sq. ft (4451 sq. m).

Sir Joseph Banks Building   Opened in 1990 to house the Centre for Economic Botany. Fully earth-covered (by terraced gardens) – a British first. Designed with energy conservation in mind: insulation is provided by surrounding soil; a heat pump exchanges heat with ground water to cool the building in summer and warm it in winter.

These succulent 'living stones' (Lithops) are camouflaged to look like their dry stony habitat

Other display houses at Kew each provide a single environment. The Temperate House is dry, with a winter temperature of 45-52°F (7-11°C). The Palm House is more humid and much hotter – with summer temperatures maintained at above 72°F (22°C). The major function of the Alpine House is to protect plants from rain and maintain an even temperature just above freezing.

There are other, even more specialised conditions in the Alpine House: the central refrigerated bench is divided into two sections to provide homes for plants from both the Arctic and the Equator. In the Arctic, daylight lasts up to 24 hours during the summer, decreasing to 24 hours of continuous darkness in mid-winter. At Kew, this is simulated by the provision of tungsten lamps attached to a timer – the extra lamplight that mimics summer is gradually decreased as the months go by. By these methods, northern plants such as *Primula scandinavica*, which in the past have been very difficult to grow for more than one year, have been cultivated successfully.

By contrast, on mountains close to the Equator, plants experience summer every day and winter every night, as well as being subject to a constant, equally divided day and night of 12 hours each. On the Alpine House's refrigerated bench, the temperature in the sand around the pots of Equatorial plants increases from 41°F (5°C) at night to 70°F (21°C) during the day, and sodium lamps above this section provide light of the correct wavelength and duration. Plants from the South American Andes and the mountains of Lesotho, Tasmania and Mexico are just some of the species grown successfully under this regime.

Grouping plants according to their natural environment can highlight similar adaptations to habitat by plants from different families. A very good example of this can be seen in plants from arid areas on show in the desert zone of the Princess of Wales Conservatory. Whether they originate in the deserts of Africa or those of America, these plants frequently have the same distinctive characteristics: they are often succulents (i.e. they have thick, fleshy parts); they sometimes have waxy coatings; and their leaves are either absent or reduced to spines.

Other factors influencing the arrangement of the collections include the plants' soil requirements (in the Alpine House) and their geographical origins (in the Palm and Temperate houses). Geographical displays bring together plants from one continent or island, showing a sample of the vegetation of a particular region.

How to create an environment

Most of the plants held in the glasshouses at Kew require very specialised environments. To meet these needs, each glasshouse incorporates a variety of systems, ranging from simple manually operated vents to complex computer-controlled screens, vents, lights and misting apparatus.

Because the tap water at Kew contains high levels of minerals that can have an adverse effect on growth, all the glasshouse plants are given rainwater. This is held in vast tanks – for example,

the one in the Princess of Wales Conservatory can hold up to 60,000 gallons, enough water to last about two weeks if no rain falls. This is supplemented by de-ionised water as necessary.

The misting systems in some of the glasshouses – necessary to maintain the correct humidity – could pose a health problem: various highly infectious bacteria, such as the ones responsible for Legionnaire's disease, can be spread in fine water droplets. To ensure that all

potentially harmful bacteria are killed, all the water used at Kew for maintaining humidity is filtered carefully and treated with ultraviolet light.

Heating is supplied to all the houses by gas-fired boilers – those for the Palm House are located some distance away, in the yard on the opposite side of the pond. Each boiler can also burn oil in the event of a shortage of gas, and enough oil is stored to keep the boilers going over winter.

Around the world in one house!

The Temperate House is built with its main axis running from north to south. By arranging the plants on a geographic plan, the variations in the levels of incoming light and in the conditions in different parts of the house can be taken into account. Thus, African and Mediterranean plants – such as the bird-of-paradise flower *(Strelitzia reginae)*, Cretan date palm *(Phoenix theophrastii)* and dragon tree *(Dracaena draco)* – have been placed in the south wing to take advantage of the best winter light. In the south octagon, where there is good ventilation and a very freely draining soil, you will find characteristic plants from the South African Cape, including ericas, proteas and leucodendrons.

The centre block, dominated by the Chilean wine palm *(Jubaea chilensis)*, contains mainly Central and South American plants, with a few from Australasia. The balcony encircling the centre block allows visitors to get a bird's-eye view of the impressive bunya-bunya pine *(Araucaria bidwillii)* and the New Zealand tree ferns *(Dicksonia* spp.).

Tree ferns viewed from above

The latter, coming from deep forest, can survive the lower light intensity at the northern end of the centre block. Displayed in the north octagon are plants from various islands in the South Pacific.

In the northern wing are the Asiatic plants. These are less dependent than the African species on high light levels and thus are not affected too much by the low levels of a British winter. Here, the Japanese banana (*Musa bajoo*), tender rhododendrons from New Guinea, and an oak – *Quercus bambusifolia* – found in China and North Vietnam, intermingle with many other interesting species.

The Chilean wine palm was raised from seed collected in the Andes in 1846 and is now over 17 metres tall

The Southern Hemisphere in Sussex

At Wakehurst Place, the plants are also arranged geographically, as well as according to their horticultural requirements. Groups found only in Australasia and South America, such as the protea family (e.g. the Chilean fire bush, *Embothrium* sp.) and the leptospermums, are grown in the Heath and Southern Hemisphere gardens. Asian plantings, such as the well-established collection of rhododendrons, are located in Westwood Valley. There are many trees from North America in the Arboretum, including the mountain redwood *Sequoiadendron giganteum*, which are concentrated in Horsebridge Woods.

A number of Wakehurst's collections have been designated 'national collections' by the National Council for the Conservation of Plants and Gardens (NCCPG). This means that the staff are responsible for assembling as comprehensive a collection of species and cultivars as possible and making this available to other botanists and horticulturists. The Wakehurst NCCPG national collections are:

♦ the hypericums, found in the Specimen Beds to the south and west of the Mansion.

♦ the southern beeches *(Nothofagus)* in Coates' Wood, including *N. glauca, N. alpina* and other species rarely seen in cultivation.

♦ the birches *(Betula)* in Bethlehem Wood.

Which plants to keep?

It is costly to collect plants from the remote regions of the world and keep them in protected, often artificial environments. However, all the plants on view in the gardens at Kew are there for a scientific reason – and not just because they look pretty.

One major factor in a plant's inclusion in Kew's collection is its scientific interest. For example, the cycads – sometimes known as the 'plant dinosaurs' – which can be seen in the Palm House, are among the most primitive seed-bearing plants. In recent years, the palm and aroid collections have been increased as a result of work currently being undertaken by botanists in the Herbarium (*see* Chapter 3).

There is also a very active research group studying orchids, but this is not the only reason why the size of Kew's collection has now reached some 1700 species. As well as its scientific work on this group, Kew provides a refuge for 123 orchid species now endangered in their natural habitats (*see* Chapter 4).

Other plants are kept because of their educational value. In the Palm and Temperate houses, you can see examples of tropical plants that have been cultivated for their value to humanity as sources of many of our common foods and raw materials: cocoa, oranges, rubber, balsa wood.

Which plants to send?

Over the years, Kew has played an important role in the spread of many plants around the world. One of the prime examples is the Para rubber plant (*Hevea brasiliensis*), collected from its native habitat in Brazil in 1876 and sent, via Kew, to South-east Asia, which now produces most of the world's natural rubber. Today, lists of rare or economically important seeds are regularly sent to other botanic gardens and national collections so that they can share the responsibility of holding endangered species.

Kew's plant collection is also used as a source of research material, with plants exchanged with other botanic gardens, scientific institutes and universities for a whole range of studies. For instance, one organisation is screening plants for bitter principles and sweetening agents for food use; plants from the rose family – the Rosaceae – are being used to breed new characteristics into stone fruits; and the lectins produced by members of the pea and bean family, the Leguminosae, are being employed in studies on blood grouping.

Endangered tropical orchids are cultivated and propagated in the nurseries

Learning from disaster

When a storm of hurricane proportions hit southern Britain without warning on the night of 16 October 1987, Kew lost many historic and well-beloved trees. The situation was much worse at Wakehurst Place, where three-quarters of the collection was damaged in some way and about 55 per cent of all exotic trees were lost.

Some good did come from this misfortune. The gaps left by fallen and damaged trees made new plantings possible so that the collection on view to the public could be more representative. In addition, some of the new vistas left by the missing trees have added interest, and some of the timber was made into souvenirs (to sell for Kew's benefit).

However, the ones who 'benefited' most from the storm were the researchers in the anatomy and biochemistry sections in the Jodrell Laboratory (**see** Chapter 3). Without the storm, the great array of species that were suddenly available for study under the microscope would have remained unexamined.

taken to aid identification. Sections from the trunks were examined to see if the widths of the rings (indicating growth) had changed in times of air pollution, as a result of the Clean Air Act of 1956 and, perhaps, because of acid rain. It is hoped that, in this way, certain tree species can be identified that will be suitable for monitoring the progress of air pollution abatement. To help horticulturists choose the right specimens for the right locations, Kew's anatomists also hope to discover which trees do best in high winds and in which soils.

As for Kew's biochemists, they are enthusiastic about the tremendous potential for research into the wide range of chemicals stored in the trees' roots, bark and trunks.

Exceptionally (since such ferocious weather is only supposed to affect southern Britain every 200 years), the storm early in 1990 caused yet further damage, with windspeeds exceeding those of the 1987 'hurricane'. Because it was winter, the evergreens were worst

Measurements of root systems of fallen trees can be used in planning future plantings

Anatomists systematically photographed and measured root systems, which will aid their work on tree root spread that can cause damage to buildings. Roots were also collected, extremely thin slices (sections) made and photomicrographs

affected, with nearly 200 mature trees at Kew and at Wakehurst Place added to the previous toll. This continuing loss of cover exposes the two arboreta to even greater damage should further storms occur.

3
Understanding the plant kingdom

Only a few of the visitors to Kew Gardens realise that the collection of plants that they enjoy seeing is, first and foremost, a scientific resource. The living plants and preserved material collected on expeditions provide the basis for a wide-ranging research programme with the aim of increasing our understanding of the plant kingdom – not least to discover how to keep it safe from destruction and how to use it sensibly for the benefit of humanity.

The Herbarium: cataloguing the world's plants

In the Herbarium at Kew, botanists study plants from all over the world in order to identify and name them and to provide methods of helping other people recognise the plants around them.

It is here that dried specimens end their journey – and today, the main collection comprises some six million seed plants, ferns and larger fungi. Dried plants retain many characteristics of the living specimens but take up a lot less space and need far less looking after. Each one

that arrives at the Herbarium is accompanied by full field notes, giving details of features that may have been lost on drying, such as petal colour and scent, as well as other information about the plant not evident from the specimen, such as its size, habitat and uses by local people. This combination of dried specimen and field notes can provide almost as much information as the living plant itself.

The Herbarium's collection of fungi is the largest, richest and most important in the world, containing over 600,000

Comprehensive field notes on fungi provide researchers with details that would not be evident from the preserved specimen

specimens – mushrooms, toadstools, cup fungi and examples of stem and leaf fungal diseases. When collected on expeditions, fungi are dried but not pressed as this would destroy their overall shape.

New specimens of all types of plants arrive at Kew at a rate of about 45,000 a year. Before entering the main Herbarium building, they are all deep-frozen for two days to ensure that any pests are killed. Each one is then allocated to a botanist for identification.

Telling one plant from another

Taxonomy is a practical science, used to distinguish, name and arrange plants and other organisms in a logical way, and it is a prerequisite for any biological study. When an unidentified flowering plant or fern arrives at the Herbarium, it is usually fairly easy to assign it to the

A herbarium sheet of the Brazilian plant, Amburana cearensis

correct family, using obvious characteristics of flowers, fruits and foliage. It is then sent to the taxonomist dealing with that family, who will discover what genus it belongs to and what species it is. Studies of the plant's structure, its chromosomes and its biochemical constituents can provide additional information to be used in its identification. This process of identifying a plant from its most general characteristics to its most specific – from family to genus to species – and arranging it in a particular system is called 'systematic classification'.

When taxonomists begin the identification of a fungus, they look at the size, shape and colour of the above-ground fruiting body, as well as any colour changes that occur when the flesh of this is exposed to air. The fruiting body's smell and, in some cases, its taste, as well as the fungus's habitat, are all noted. Sometimes, for accurate identification, the fungal spores have to be examined under the microscope; their size, form, ornamentation and chemical characteristics can often provide vital clues.

Storage and arrangement

After it has been identified and named, a plant is mounted on a herbarium sheet so that it can be studied easily and will not be damaged in storage. It is carefully arranged on the sheet so that its characteristic features are clearly displayed, with both sides of leaves and flowers showing. Delicate flowers are protected by translucent paper flaps, and parts that have been detached for study are placed in an attached envelope. A label gives details of the plant's name,

who collected it, the collector's number and any field notes. Then the sheet is returned to the botanist, who will place it in the correct sequence in the collection.

Additional plant material – especially complex or delicate flowers such as those of orchids and cacti – is stored in 'herbarium spirit', an alcohol-based mixture containing a preservative. Material stored in this way retains its three-dimensional shape for future study. There are also separate collections of seeds, fruits and other dry bulky material, held in boxes.

Before plants can be used as reference sources for the identification of new specimens, they must be arranged in such a way that the information can actually be retrieved. In the Herbarium, plants are placed in the correct families and, within those, in the correct genus. Within each genus, however, they are arranged geographically. Thus, in the Herbarium there is an attempt to have a readily accessible, representative sample of the world's vegetation, highlighting its diversity and distribution.

Taxonomy at the microscopic level

Pollen grains can vary a great deal in structure and appearance from species to species, and these characteristics can be used to identify a particular one. Under powerful electron microscopes, the Herbarium's Palynology Unit can survey a pollen grain's surface ornamentation, the position of its apertures and the arrangement of layers in its walls. Pollen identification carried out by the Unit has been used to determine different types of honey, as

well as the sources of objects contaminated by pollen grains – for instance, to aid forensic scientists in obtaining criminal evidence.

Another aspect of the Unit's work is the identification of fossilised pollen grains. The complex substance that makes up the grains' walls is very resistant to decay, and as a result, grains are preserved in the soil over many millenia. When such grains have been identified, researchers can discover which types of plants formed the vegetation of a particular area at a particular time and can look for evidence of climatic change.

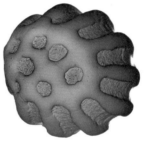

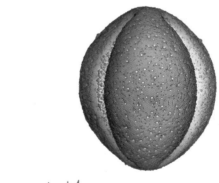

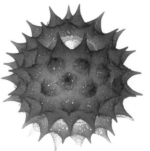

Scanning electron micrographs of different pollen grains: top – common milkwort, Polygala vulgaris; centre – Christmas rose, Helleborus niger; bottom – daisy, Bellis perennis

The characteristic wood structure of beech (Fagus sylvatica) can be seen in this cross-section of a branch

The Jodrell Laboratory: experimental research

In the north-east corner of the Gardens, close to the Alpine House, stands the Jodrell Laboratory, the site of much experimental research. In contrast to the Herbarium, where researchers are mainly concerned with the external appearance of plants, work in the Jodrell is directed towards their microscopic and chemical characteristics.

These micrographs show the surface features of Haworthia setata (left) and Aloe dawei (right). The waxy surfaces of these plants from the desert regions of southern Africa reduce water loss

Plant anatomy: the surface and beyond

Using light and electron microscopes, researchers can examine plants at various magnifications to study their tissues or even individual cells. The Jodrell's Anatomy Section now has a reference collection of some 70,000 microscope slides of sections sliced through the wood, leaves and stems of plants. This provides a basis for systematic research and also a means of identifying unknown species by their microscopic structure.

As well as their internal structure, plants' surface features may provide clues to relationships between species. The aloes and haworthias, for example, have characteristic stomas, tiny pores in the outer layer of leaves. Because hybrids occasionally show some of the surface features inherited from both parents, it may be possible to determine a hybrid's origins by examining these.

The production of seeds by a plant is dependent on three processes: first, pollination; then, fertilisation of the ovule (embryo sac) by fusion of the female gamete (egg cell) with a male gamete from a pollen grain to produce an embryo; and finally, development and

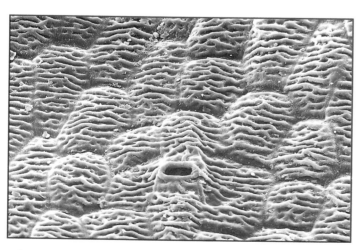

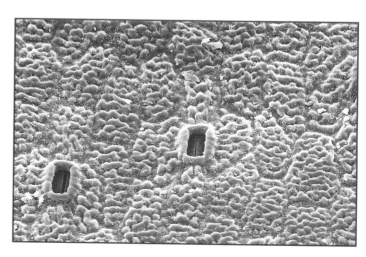

maturation of the seed. Sometimes plants have incompatibility systems that prevent pollination or fertilisation unless suitable sources of pollen can be found. In the Transmission Electron Microscope (TEM) Unit at the Jodrell, the stigmas, styles and ovaries of flowers are studied, both for taxonomic purposes and to understand how the ovule is fertilised so that clues can be found about the point at which incompatibility systems operate. This is particularly important for threatened species, where the production of seed is vital.

Physiology: structure and function

The timber trees of South-east Asia, harvested directly from their natural habitat, provide a large proportion of the world's tropical hardwoods. However, few of them can be grown on managed plantations because their often large and fleshy seeds, which are produced unpredictably once every three to seven years, die quickly if they are dried or stored moist without adequate oxygen. Thus they cannot be transported or stored from harvest to planting.

Researchers in the Jodrell's Physiology Section are investigating these and other plants with such 'recalcitrant' seeds to discover how seed survival is controlled

and how this control can be manipulated so that tropical hardwood forests can be managed as a renewable and ecologically stable resource.

The Physiology Section is also involved in the work of the World Seed Bank at Wakehurst Place (*see* Chapter 4).

The Madagascan periwinkle (Catharanthus roseus) is an important source of drugs used to treat leukaemia

Biochemistry: plants as chemical factories

In addition to carbohydrates, lipids and proteins, plants produce many other chemicals, including some whose biological functions are unknown. These compounds – called secondary metabolites – may have a physiological effect either in the plant itself or on other organisms, possibly protecting the plant by deterring predators such as insects, or inhibiting competing plant species. This biological activity can be harnessed for the benefit of people – in, say, agriculture or medicine – and because these secondary metabolites are

Anti-AIDS research

The legume **Castanospermum australe** – the Moreton Bay chestnut – is native to the rainforests of New South Wales and Queensland and is now a common street tree in Australia. Its seeds and foliage are toxic to livestock, and the substance responsible was found to be a compound now called 'castanospermine'.

Moreton Bay chestnut seeds were first described by one of Sir Joseph Banks' plant collectors

During screening assays, castanospermine was found to reduce the infectivity of the virus that causes AIDS. Projecting from the surface of this virus are structures, made up of glycoproteins (sugar and protein), which are involved in cell recognition. The newly discovered compound is thought to modify these structures, and as a result, the virus is rendered non-infectious because it cannot fuse with its target: one of the white blood cells that are involved in the body's immune system. Castanospermine may also be of use against diabetes and some cancers.

At first, it was thought that the only source of castanospermine was the seed of the Moreton Bay chestnut. However, an examination in the Herbarium of the taxonomic descriptions and illustrations of related species worldwide showed that the flowers and fruits of species in the genus **Alexa**, confined to the rain-

Studying herbarium sheets of Alexa

forests of Central America, closely resembled the Australian species. A pod of an **Alexa** species, which had been stored in the Herbarium for 40 years, was found to contain the compound, as well as others of potential medicinal interest.

This example clearly shows the importance of protecting plants that have no apparent value – which, indeed, may be poisonous – but subsequently turn out to have useful or even vital properties.

often found only in one group of closely related plants, they can also be useful taxonomic markers.

In the Biochemistry Section, researchers looking into this aspect of plants direct their work not only towards species of interest to other researchers in the Jodrell and the Herbarium. They also study certain plants (and related species) that have been traditionally used in herbal medicine, and those that grow abundantly, but for which there is, as yet, no apparent use – for instance, 'weeds' and aquatic plants. Extracts from these plants are tested for their activity in a number of biological systems. For instance, a chemical may be screened against enzymes implicated in disease, such as glycosidase; against disease-causing organisms, such as the malarial parasite; or against pests, including locusts and bruchid beetles. One such screening has shown that certain plant extracts can reduce nematode (eelworm) damage to plant roots. If any activity is detected, the compounds responsible are isolated and their structures determined using

sophisticated methods such as nuclear magnetic resonance and mass spectrometry.

If an unusual compound is found only in two species within a family, it is quite likely that those two plants are descended from a common ancestor and thus are closely related. Alternatively, certain combinations of compounds may be peculiar to particular species. For instance, the aloes contain some 80 phenolic compounds, of which only 20 have been identified. These compounds provide a 'chemical fingerprint' characteristic of each species or group of species, and a hybrid between such plants may contain the 'fingerprints' of the parent plants.

Cytogenetics: inside the nucleus

In the Cytogenetics Section, researchers study chromosomes, which are located in the nucleus of every cell of a plant (and of other living things). Chromosomes are made up of protein and DNA, and the latter comprises the cell's genetic material. The chromosomes with their DNA encode a blueprint that

Interesting compounds with biological activity are isolated from plant extracts using a series of different purification stages

During cell division, chromosomes contract and become visible under the light microscope. Each pair of chromosomes has a specific pattern of bands of highly repetitive DNA, shown here fluorescing with DAPI stain

will define all of a plant's characteristics, although these may be modified by environmental factors.

In general, each plant species has a certain number of chromosomes (although there are exceptions), and these, in turn, have a characteristic appearance in terms of shape, size, position of constrictions and light and dark bands (seen after staining). This unique appearance is known as the karyotype, and karyotypes are important in taxonomic and evolutionary studies, which seek to discover how species are related. Cytogenetic research is also valuable to plant breeders, because it may indicate the probability of achieving viable hybrids in plant crosses. Many of the problems under investigation in this part of the Jodrell relate to a group of plants known as the petaloid monocotyledons, which include the daffodils, aloes and tradescantias.

Another area of research is 'population cytogenetics' – the study of chromosome variability occurring within and between populations of particular species. Such studies, combined with our knowledge of breeding systems and ecology, are important when dealing with scattered or dwindling populations of threatened plant species. They can also be used to assess the ways in which plant populations cope with changes in the environment, as well as how new species develop.

Molecular biosystematics: deep into DNA

The Molecular Biosystematics Section will be looking even closer at plant DNA. Some sequences of DNA are so specific to particular plant species or genera that they could be used as a means of identification, equivalent to a 'genetic fingerprint'. However, there are so few of these sequences among the total amount of DNA that searching for them is rather like looking for a needle in a haystack. As yet, only small amounts of these sequences can be extracted, but they have great potential both as diagnostic tools and as 'hooks' to 'fish out' similar sequences in related species.

The Section is currently developing a system by which small amounts of interesting DNA sequences can be bulked up for detailed study. In time, this will allow scientists in the Jodrell to identify particular plants and to discover how closely related they are, a factor of considerable importance in deciding which plants to use for breeding purposes. For example, certain rare orchids will only produce viable seed if cross-pollinated with relatives that are genetically distinct; self-pollination, or brother-sister matings, are infertile and therefore useless.

Molecular biosystematics could help to identify subtle genetic differences in similar-looking plants, and this, in turn, could influence the breeder's choice of plants to use for hybridisation. The increase in viable offspring that is likely to result will be very useful in orchid conservation, because these hybrids between only subtly different forms should succeed as well as the parents in the wild.

Economic botany: new uses for plants

At present, people in the developed world are dependent on a tiny proportion of the plant kingdom for

People in developing countries rely on many different plants during their daily lives

food, medicine, clothing, building materials and so on. In the developing world, many indigenous peoples are far better acquainted with the potential uses of plants and often utilise a large number of the species available in their immediate environment. Before these species disappear from the wild, we must assess and document their properties and, whenever possible, find a method of conserving these plants in the long term.

We have already looked at a number of ways in which the research at Kew's Herbarium and at the Jodrell Laboratory is being employed to discover new uses for plants. But there are other, even more practical, things that can be done do alleviate the problems facing humanity.

Botanists are studying plants that are able to grow in this dry salty part of Botswana

Plants for dry areas

The long-term solution to the problems of famine and poverty in the arid regions of the world – such as in the Sahel, the part of Africa around the Sahara that is gradually turning into desert – will ultimately depend on the growing of plants that have very specialised

Photo: Peter Johnson/NHPA

rattan, Calamus ovoideus, growing in rainforest in Sri Lanka

adaptations enabling them to withstand the shortage of water. However, until 1981, information on these plants was not readily available. It was in that year that the Survey of Economic Plants for Arid and Semi-Arid Lands (SEPASAL) was set up, to provide a computer database of plants growing in dry areas, either wild or as minor crops, and with the aim of answering the questions 'Which plants can be used for which purposes?' and 'Where do they grow?'

Information for the database comes from botanical books and journals and from herbarium sheets, which provide valuable details of the form and distribution of different plants. The data for each plant presently entered into the computer includes its scientific name, a brief description of its form, its possible toxicity, the environment in which it grows and its distribution. The economic uses of the plant are coded in up to 600 categories so that the relevant part of the plant and how it is used can be determined.

The SEPASAL database has provided answers to many enquiries from international organisations, governmental agencies, universities, charities and interested members of the public. For example, it has come up with plants suitable for reforestation in the Indian state of Rajasthan, methods of tapping gum arabic, and the uses of watermelons as animal feed.

Replacements for wild plants

Another economic area in which Kew has become involved is, perhaps rather surprisingly, the cane furniture industry. Cane furniture is made from rattans, members of the palm family, which are worth some £1500 million on the international market. At present, most rattans are harvested directly from the wild – in the rainforests of the Old World tropics – and local shortages occur due to overexploitation and deforestation.

In some parts of Indonesia, however, rattans are cultivated in secondary forests or on smallholdings. These are the multi-stemmed, small-diameter canes that are wrapped around the furniture's sturdy frames. Unfortunately, no large-diameter canes, required for the frames, have so far been successfully cultivated, and they must still be harvested from the wild. If a suitable large-cane species can be found, it could be planted in forests to increase the natural complement of rattans, or in previously unused forest to provide a cash return which may decrease the threat from logging.

A botanist from Kew has been surveying rattans throughout South-east Asia to find out which species are present and assess their suitability as plantation crops. He has also been studying the biology of these climbing palms, to discover more about their response to light, their nutritional requirements and the effect of competition from other plants. All this information will be used to decide how to grow rattans effectively in plantations.

Computerised wood

Another database at Kew is of both economic and environmental importance.

Different woods that are used for the same purpose by different peoples around the world – for example, to make axe handles or musical instruments – often have properties in common, which are dependent on the wood structure. The various structural characteristics of tropical woods – as seen in the Anatomy Section's microscope slide collection, prepared from specimens in museums at Kew and elsewhere – are being coded and entered on a computer alongside the uses to which these woods have been put. From this database, it will be possible to predict which woods may be of use for a particular purpose simply by finding out the woods with a similar set of characteristics which have already been used in this way.

By identifying underexploited but potentially valuable woods, our dependence on a few timber species – some of which are already endangered – can be reduced, and new industries can be encouraged in developing parts of the world.

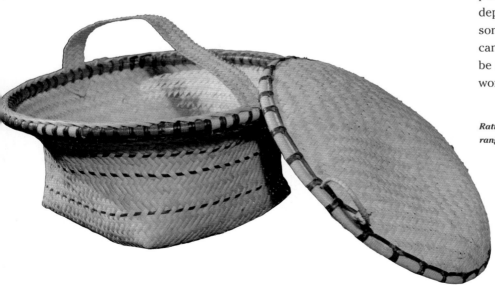

Rattan canes are used in rainforest areas to make a range of different baskets and mats

4

Saving plants from extinction

The natural vegetation of many parts of the world is rapidly disappearing because of habita destruction for peasant agriculture and because of the overexploitation of 'economic' (commercia plant species. However, if we are to find out the true value of a particular region – in terms of it plants and animals and their potential – we first have to discover which species are present. Th Floras compiled by Kew botanists – such as the recent work done in the forests of South-east Asi and the mountains of Brazil – provide a vital basis for the conservation of these vulnerable areas.

Botanists and horticulturists from Kew also work closely with their opposite numbers in botanic gardens and nature reserves around the world. Important work is done in Britain, too – to police the import and export of rare plants, increase the numbers of threatened foreign species, conserve native plants, and, through the World Seed Bank at Wakehurst Place, preserve the diversity of the plant kingdom.

International links

Since its inception, Kew has had strong ties with other countries. From the transport of breadfruit from Tahiti to the West Indies on that troubled ship, the *Bounty*, to the expeditions sent out from Kew today, botanists and horticulturists have brought plants back to the gardens and laboratories by the Thames. Now, however, much more emphasis is placed on the importance of conserving plants *in situ*, and to this end, Kew is in the forefront of the movement to develop nature reserves and botanic gardens in various parts of the world.

One such is the Limbe Botanic Garden in Cameroon. This is one of the richest

A representative collection of African palms is cultivated at the Limbe Botanic Garden

...ountries in tropical Africa in the ...iversity of plant species found there, ...ith rainforest stretching from sea-level ...o mountain-side. Founded by the ...ermans in 1892, the botanic garden was ...ited on the coast at Limbe, near ...ameroon Mountain, and came into ...ritish hands after World War I, but by ...he 1930s, it had fallen into disrepair.

...ifty years later, a Kew staff member ...isited the garden as part of a team from ...he Overseas Development ...dministration, to see if it could be ...ehabilitated and to assess local ...ainforest sites for their scientific interest ...nd their status as genetic resources. ...ollowing that visit, it was agreed with ...he Cameroon government that the ...otanic garden will be used to exhibit ...seful, ornamental and scientifically ...nteresting plants, primarily with the aim ...f educating local visitors in the value of plant life and the need for its conservation. It will also be the site of a major living collection of African palms, which will act as a gene bank. In addition, two areas of forest nearby – at Etinde (Small Cameroon Mountain) and Mabeta-Moliwe – are to be set aside as nature reserves. Kew will be actively involved in training Cameroonian horticultural students, as well as providing technical assistance and facilities.

Controlling the commerce in endangered species

The continued survival of many wild plants is threatened by, among other things, overcollecting for commercial reasons. Plants such as cyclamen, orchids and cacti are taken from the wild in great quantities by the horticultural trade, with particular species – almost always rare ones – being highly prized (and coveted) by some unscrupulous specialist growers and collectors.

In an effort to conserve such plants, the Convention on International Trade in Endangered Species of Wild Flora and Fauna (CITES) was set up in the early 1970s to control and monitor trade in rare and threatened plants and animals. CITES has now been endorsed by nearly 100 signatory countries. As the designated UK scientific authority for plants, Kew advises the Department of the Environment (DOE) – the licensing authority – on these matters. Trade in wild plants on the verge of extinction is banned; the import and export of less threatened species are monitored closely.

23

The dust-like seeds of orchids, which can sometimes be difficult to germinate, are cultured on nutrient jelly under controlled conditions

Propagation: safety in numbers

Conventional methods of propagation are used at Kew for a wide variety of plants. However, when plants are difficult to regenerate by these means or have to be multiplied rapidly because they are endangered in the wild, the most up-to-date technology of micropropagation is employed.

Using a binocular microscope, a scientist cuts out tiny pieces of plant tissue and sterilises their surfaces to eliminate disease-causing organisms; alternatively, seeds may be used. The tissue or seed is then cultured in sterile flasks containing a jelly-like medium with all the nutrients needed for growth, as well as plant hormones to overcome dormancy or induce numerous shoots to develop. The flasks are incubated at the relatively high temperature of 72°F (22°C).

When shoots have grown, they are separated from the original tissue and transferred to a different nutrient medium to initiate root formation. When the shoots – now plantlets – have reached a suitable size, they are again transferred, this time to sterile compost, and grown on in a glasshouse. Since they experience very high humidity in the flasks, the plantlets have to be gently weaned back to normal glasshouse conditions.

The list of threatened plants that have been successfully propagated in this way is a long one, but it includes: the tropical epiphytic orchid, *Epidendrum ilense*, from Ecuador, thought to be extinct in the wild; the tropical ferns *Angiopteris boivinii* from the Seychelles and *Lindsaea odorata* from Sabah, part of Malaysia; the succulent *Aloe patersonii* from Zaïre; and the carnivorous pitcher plants *Darlingtonia californica* from California and *Nepenthes khasiana* from southern India.

The lady's slipper orchid is almost extinct in the wild in Britain

Saving orchids

Orchids have always been favourites of Kew's researchers and gardeners – not to mention visitors to Kew. The origins of the orchid herbarium date back to the first part of the nineteenth century; and Kew now also has a large number of orchid flowers preserved in spirit, an excellent collection of illustrations and one of the world's largest living orchid collections.

Conservation of these beautiful plants also has a high profile. The purpose of the Sainsbury Orchid Project is to find ways of raising rare and endangered British and European terrestrial orchids. There have been several successes, among them propagating from seed the lady's slipper orchid **(Cypripedium calceolus)**, which has been reduced to one individual clump in the British Isles. Some of the resulting seedlings will eventually be returned to the wild.

Brazil and its plant riches

Since 1974, Kew has been sending staff members to Bahia, a state of great natural beauty and considerable scientific importance in north-east Brazil. It encompasses a wide range of vegetation types: coastal rainforest, transitional grassland, savannah woodland, shrubby **campo rupestre** in the mountains, and **caatinga** thorn scrub in the semi-arid north, where the predominant legumes used daily by local people may have great potential as arid-land crops.

Kew's researchers, working with their counterparts from the Cocoa Research Institute in Bahia and the University of São Paulo, have concentrated mainly on the **campo rupestre** and **caatinga** regions. Publications resulting from their work include **The Grasses of Bahia, The Legumes of Bahia** and a Flora of Mucugê.

Kew's policy of concentrating on individual sites or family groups of plants

ensures that the information gathered is published quickly for use in conservation and, more broadly, by decision-makers in the country. For example, the Flora of Mucugê covers a small site of **campo rupestre**-type vegetation within the mountain region known as the Chapada Diamantina. The shallow stony soil there supports mainly grasslands and upland

Campo rupestre-type vegetation covers the rocky uplands of eastern Brazil

swamps, with a few small trees and shrubs and innumerable herbaceous species; there is also a high proportion of endemic species. Partly as a result of Kew's work, the Chapada Diamantina has recently been designated a national park by the Brazilian government.

Endangered plants from the Canary Islands are grown in the protected environment of the Princess of Wales Conservatory

Island flora

The plant life of islands often develops in a very specialised, unique way because of its remoteness from other plants. These are also quite fragile ecosystems, more vulnerable to overexploitation, disease and changes from habitat modifications than those found on the mainland. Much work at Kew has, therefore, been directed towards preserving island floras, and among the examples that visitors can see, there are plants from the Canary Islands and Madagascar in the Princess of Wales Conservatory.

Micropropagation has been used to increase the numbers of the succulent *Opuntia echios* from the Galapagos Islands, *Limonium* species from the Canary Islands and *Trichodesma scottii* from Socotra in the Indian Ocean. The population of the extremely rare *Nesocodon mauritianus*, found only by a remote waterfall in Mauritius, was

increased by the micropropagation of seeds. And there are now more specimens of *Commidendrum robustum* from St Helena in the south Atlantic, where a propagation unit for rare endemic plants (i.e. plants found nowhere else) was set up with the help of Kew staff.

In June 1987, the Temperate Nursery received a single unrooted shoot from the last remaining example of the café marron tree *(Ramosmania heterophylla)*

on Rodrigues Island in the southern Indian Ocean. This was induced to produce roots, and when it was established in cultivation, a second cutting was taken. Both mother and child did well, and a specimen has now been returned to the nearby island of Réunion.

Looking after our native plants

As well as providing a refuge for threatened exotic species from other countries, Kew is concerned with protecting the native plant species of the British Isles. Many of these are under threat through loss of habitat due to the pressure on available land from agriculture, industry and housing.

Throughout the Gardens at Kew, there are small patches of British wild flowers. In particular, the area around Queen Charlotte's Cottage, donated by Queen Victoria in celebration of her Jubilee in 1898, has been set aside as a reserve for British wild plants.

Many more British species are to be seen at Kew's West Sussex annexe, Wakehurst Place. Examples of native bog, marshland and water plants are displayed in the Water Garden, and small sites have been planted with terrestrial orchids such as the Jersey orchid *(Orchis laxiflora)*. Part of the mature woodland on the estate has been designated a Site of Special Scientific Interest, and two species found there are particularly rare: the Tunbridge filmy fern *(Hymenophyllum tunbrigense)* and the violet helleborine *(Epipactis purpurata)*.

Another part of the Wakehurst Place estate – the Loder Valley – is a reserve for plants of the Sussex Weald. It encompasses three major habitats: woodland, wetland and meadow. On the Weald, all of these are subject to severe pressure from intensive agriculture, and their characteristic plants and animals are being lost.

Queen Charlotte's Cottage grounds are managed to provide habitats for British native plants

The World Seed Bank

A cold, dry storage facility close to the Tudor Mansion at Wakehurst Place holds the seeds of over 2500 species of flowering plants – one of the world's largest collections – providing protected storage for material of international value as well as innumerable specimens for research.

Following collection from the wild, seeds are sorted and cleaned to remove debris, and a sample is X-rayed to check that they are intact and do not contain insect pests. After this processing, the seeds are dried by exposure to low relative humidity at 59°F (15°C) and then stored in air-tight containers within a room kept at deep-freeze temperatures. Being frozen in this way ensures that their lifespans will be greatly enhanced – possibly to as much as 20,000 years in species such as barley. Collections held by the World Seed Bank are monitored from time to time to check that the seeds remain viable.

On expeditions, seeds are collected from as many types of plants as possible in any one area – first, because it is impossible to know which ones will prove useful in the future, and second, to make sure that a broad genetic base is obtained. However, care is also taken to leave sufficient seed to allow the plant population to regenerate in future years. The collectors pay particular attention to grasses and legumes (plants that produce edible seed pods, such as peas and beans) because, based on previous experience, they know that both these groups of plants are likely to be useful. They also collect seeds from plants that are utilised by the local people, such as those with medicinal qualities.

A collector from the Seed Bank collecting samples in Botswana

Using information gleaned from the Herbarium botanists and from computer databases such as SEPASAL (*see* Chapter 3), Kew's collectors have travelled to the countries around the Mediterranean and to the arid and semi-arid tropics (including Brazil, Botswana and Somalia) in their quest for seeds. Conserving British flora has also not been forgotten.

In recent years, the rate at which seeds have been added to the Bank has increased dramatically following the funding of two collectors devoted solely to that task. At present, they are concentrating on plants in arid and semi-arid lands such as Mexico, Australia and Morocco, sometimes having to set out at a moment's notice when news reaches them that a rare spell of rain has induced flowering and seed production in a remote desert area. In the future, remote-sensing satellites will help them to pinpoint the places where rain has fallen.

> *The genetic reservoir of the plant and animal life sharing our world provides us, I believe, with the most perfect survival kit imaginable as we face the unknown challenges of the future. It is impossible to predict which parts of the survival kit might one day be needed, yet we allow its contents to be discarded with scarcely a thought or a backward glance.*
>
> **HRH The Prince of Wales**
> *The Rainforest Lecture*

5

Spreading the word

Plants do not usually make headlines in conservation stories in the same way that animals do. Ye
we depend on plants for our very existence as well as in our daily lives – without them, there woul
be no life on earth, there would be no food, there would be no tea, no cotton, no aspirins, no tyre:
no wooden tables. These and a host of other products originate in the plant kingdom, and there ar
thousands of other plants whose value we have not yet discovered – perhaps as possible sources c
fuel or life-saving drugs – and which are threatened in the wild.
The Royal Botanic Gardens, Kew has a mission to increase the public's awareness of what plant
have to offer, and it does this through the interpretation of research, its plant collections and it
educational activities.

Sir Joseph Banks Centre for Economic Botany

This, the newest part of Kew, contains some 75,000 items that have been collected since the time of the Gardens' first official director, Sir William Hooker, who established a 'Museum of Economic Botany' in 1847 to show plant products that were 'either eminently curious or in any way serviceable to mankind'.

As well as a vast collection of the products of herbaceous plants, ranging from cloth, sunhats and poisons, to oils, jewellery and teas, there are about 28,000 samples of different woods, and

Samples of woods from all over the world are held in the economic botany collection

9000 items (zoological as well as botanical), acquired because of their reputed medicinal properties, which were donated by the Pharmaceutical Society of Great Britain in 1983.

Life', a multi-media presentation devoted to mankind's use of plant cellulose.

Pictures of beauty and knowledge

In these days of photography, it may seem odd that plants are still drawn and painted for scientific reasons. However, such botanical illustrations can show the characteristics of plants in a far clearer way than photographs.

nformation on all these specimens is eing entered into a number of omputer databases (the wood database s discussed in Chapter 3). These atalogues will offer researchers the pportunity to locate, for example, all naterial used for a particular purpose or rom a particular country, or specimens ollected by a particular person in a particular year or region. Other nformation is contained in a library of ooks and journals concerned with conomic botany, and a bibliographic latabase with over 130,000 references, pdated weekly.

The items within the collections will also be examined and tested. This has already led to some striking discoveries. For instance, a herbarium specimen of the poisonous *Strychnos nux-vomica*, collected in Sri Lanka in 1675, was found still to contain ten alkaloids despite its great age; and an investigation of the chemical composition of pine resins has enabled researchers to identify the botanical origins of pine resins found in archaeological deposits.

Outside the Centre, the planting theme is 'Plants for People', with examples of plants used for food, medicine, shelter, clothing and decoration. This economic botany theme is continued inside, with displays of plants in the glass-roofed concourse and major exhibitions in the exhibition hall, such as the 'Thread of

Botanical artists capture the fine detail of living plants

Over 800 plant paintings are displayed in the Marianne North Gallery

Kew holds a collection of approximately 175,000 botanical illustrations, dating back over 200 years. In addition, a team of freelance illustrators is responsible for creating many new illustrations every year. However, the most famous collection of botanical paintings within Kew is contained in the Marianne North Picture Gallery. This comprises 832 oil paintings of plants, animals, insects and general scenes from the many countries the intrepid Marianne North visited during her travels between 1871 and 1885. These were arranged by her in the gallery (which she also donated) to idiosyncratic but breathtaking effect, with all available wall space covered by these colourful works, and this is how they have remained ever since.

Plants on the printed page

After the preserved plant collections, the most important research tool for Kew's taxonomists and others is the scientific literature. In addition to the illustration collection, the Library at Kew holds one of the foremost collections of botanical texts in the world, with over 120,000 books and 3000 journals covering all of Kew's research disciplines. As well as the most up-to-date journals, it also contains much information of historical importance in its archive of the correspondence and personal papers of many of the botanists who have, over the years, been connected with Kew.

An extensive range of books and other publications is also published by or in association with Kew. As well as

scientific journals and books – such as *Kew Bulletin, Kew Magazine* and *Index Kewensis* – there are books of more general interest reflecting Kew's activities including some based on the botanical illustrations collection in the Library, as well as the ever-popular Kew calendar and guides to the Gardens and glasshouses. (*See* Further reading.)

Advising and educating others

Kew's long history as a botanic garden has meant that a vast store of expertise in plant cultivation has been accumulated. The staff in the Gardens, the Jodrell Laboratory and the

Students on the Herbarium Techniques Course learn skills ranging from plant collecting and mounting to preparation of Floras

Herbarium share this knowledge with other horticulturists and researchers around the world. For instance, between 1984 and 1986 there were research visitors from over 40 countries – over 9000 in 1986 alone. Botanists from

around the world also come to learn herbarium techniques on the Herbarium diploma course.

Members of the Gardens' staff help train students through a three-year diploma course run by Kew's School of Horticulture. Travel scholarships enable some students to visit other gardens in Britain and abroad to widen their experience of cultural conditions and plant groups. After receiving their diplomas, Kew's graduates have gone on to become, among many other things, managers of botanic gardens, lecturers at horticultural colleges, local government parks managers and landscape architects, and some have returned to Kew as members of staff. The School of Horticulture also arranges shorter periods of training for visiting horticulturists.

Members of the public have also taken advantage of Kew's educative role. Education officers provide tours and lectures on topics related to the National Curriculum, as well as advanced training for PhD students; in-service training is regularly provided for teachers, using plants as a major resource. There is also tour service for adults on topics related to Kew, and a new venture launched in 1989 is an adult education programme covering botanical and horticultural subjects related to Kew's mission. In addition, the Enquiry Unit co-ordinates replies to the many thousands of written and phoned questions, directing those on horticultural topics, those on the identification of plants and those relating to crops to the relevant departments.

Crinum northianum **from Borneo was named after Marianne North in recognition of her botanical discoveries**

6
The future

Ghillean T. Prance

Director, Royal Botanic Gardens, Kew

The future of the Royal Botanic Gardens, Kew, will be built on the strengths of our past. Althoug[h] botanists have gone out from Kew for over 200 years, expeditions still have a great man[y] undiscovered species to find, name and classify. However, as our Herbarium and Living Collection[s] continue to expand in the traditional way from the results of our expeditions, science at Kew will [be] enhanced by many new techniques.

The next decade will see the increasing use of molecular biological methods to examine plant DNA and thus add a new dimension to our taxonomic work on plants. In late 1990, construction is beginning on an extension to the Jodrell Laboratory to house molecular systematics and unite our scattered laboratories under one roof in modern and well-equipped surroundings.

As ecological problems increase in the world around us, plant conservation will play an ever-expanding role in the life of Kew. The information available in our Herbarium and Library and the skill of our horticulturists at cultivating hard-to-rear plants uniquely equips us to tackle some aspects of conservation. The rare plants that we have already reintroduced into the wild are just the beginning of what we shall be called upon to do for the restoration of destroyed ecosystems around the world. The World Seed Bank and the Living Collections comprise an abundant resource for reafforestation of the humid tropics and to combat desertification of the arid tropics.

The garden at Wakehurst Place is giving us the opportunity to expand our living collections considerably: as it recovers from the storm damage of 1987, we are rehabilitating it with an exciting trans-Asian heath garden. At Wakehurst – and especially in the Loder Valley Reserve and the part of the estate designated a 'Site of Special Scientific Interest' – we will be able to continue to practise conservation on our own doorstep.

The World Seed Bank is a repository of genetic diversity, held for future generations, as a source of plant material for breeding programmes, for pharmacological research, and as a back-up system for in situ *conservation*

An area that I hope to see developing in the future is that of the interpretation of our scientific work to the public. New 'visitor orientation centres', planned for the Main Gate and the Victoria Gate areas, will give information about the vital scientific work carried on behind the scenes at Kew, which is not generally apparent to visitors to the Gardens. Another way in which we shall increase this interpretation will be through more courses for both adults and children. Education is an important function of a botanic garden, and our new education centre in a former museum building gives us the space to increase our teaching.

The current trend at Kew is a change from being financed wholly by the government to a mixture of public and private funding. Already established are the Royal Botanic Gardens, Kew Foundation and a members' organisation – the Friends of the Royal Botanic Gardens, Kew. These two new charities are helping us to raise the funds for the new programmes on which we must embark to maintain our scientific and horticultural excellence into the twenty-first century. The work of the Foundation will enable us to add molecular biologists, arid-land researchers, seed-collectors and other scientists and horticulturists to our staff, so that we can co-operate with others to promote the better management of the earth's environment through increased knowledge and understanding of the plant kingdom – the basis of life on earth. By joining the Friends (*see* p. 35), you too can help us with this mission.

33

Resources

FURTHER READING

Books published by the Royal Botanic Gardens, Kew

The Rainforest Lecture, HRH The Prince of Wales, 1990.

The Thread of Life, 1990.

Wakehurst Place: The Culpeper Connection, Christine Stockwell, 1990.

Books published for the Royal Botanic Gardens, Kew by Her Majesty's Stationery Office

Annual Report 1987-88, Royal Botanic Gardens, Kew, 1989.

Bible Plants at Kew, F. Nigel Hepper, 1981.

Kew Gardens for Science and Pleasure, F. Nigel Hepper (ed.), 1982.

Planting a Bible Garden, F. Nigel Hepper, 1987.

A Souvenir and Guide to the Royal Botanic Gardens, Kew, 1990.

A Souvenir and Guide to Wakehurst Place, 1990.

Books published in association with the Royal Botanic Gardens, Kew

A Celebration of Flowers, Ray Desmond, Collingridge, 1987.

Eyewitness: Plant, David Burnie, Dorling Kindersley, in association with the Natural History Museum, London.

The Flowering of Kew, Richard Mabey, Century Hutchinson, 1988.

Flower Artists of Kew, William T. Stearn, Herbert Press, 1990.

The Greatest Glasshouse, Sue Minter, HMSO, 1990.

Kew Gardens Book of Indoor Plants, John Simmons (ed.), George Philip, 1988.

The Magic of Kew, James Bartholomew, Herbert Press, 1988.

Marianne North at Kew Gardens, Laura Ponsonby, Webb & Bower, 1990.

The Mediterranean Gardener, Hugo Latymer, Frances Lincoln Ltd, 1990.

Nature's Pharmacy, Christine Stockwell, Arrow Books, 1988.

Pharaoh's Flowers, F. Nigel Hepper, HMSO, 1990.

Plant Hunting for Kew, F. Nigel Hepper (ed.), HMSO, 1989.

Plants for People, Anna Lewington, Natural History Museum, 1990.

Postcards from Kew, Gwilym Lewis, HMSO, 1990.

Tree Roots and Buildings, D. F. Cutler & I. B. K. Richardson, Longman, 1989.

Vision of Eden, Marianne North, Webb & Bower, 1980.

Other books

Jungles, Edward Ayensu, Jonathan Cape Ltd, 1980.

Key Environments: Amazonia, G. T. Prance & T. E. Lovejoy, Pergamon, 1985.

Margaret Mee: In search of the flowers of the Amazon forests, Tony Morrison (ed.), Nonesuch Expeditions, 1988.

The Rainforests: A celebration, Earthlife Foundation, Barrie & Jenkins, 1989.

SOURCES OF INFORMATION

General information about Kew and Wakehurst Place – together with details of events taking place in the Gardens – can be obtained from Public Relations at Kew (tel. 081-940 1171).

Courses on a variety of horticultural, botanical and environmental topics are organised by the Education Section (tel. 081-940 1171).

VISITING THE ROYAL BOTANIC GARDENS, KEW AND WAKEHURST PLACE

Royal Botanic Gardens, Kew

HOW TO GET THERE Situated near the M3, M and South Circular roads. Nearby railwa stations – Kew Gardens (BR North London Line and District Line on the underground) and Kew Bridge (British Rail) – provide easy access. River steamers run from Westminster Pier to Kew Pier during summer months.

OPENING TIMES Gardens are open every da (except Christmas Day and New Year's Day) at 9.30 am. Closing times vary fro 4 pm to 6.30 pm on weekdays and 4 pm to 8 pm on Sundays and public holiday

FACILITIES Guides, maps, books, postcards souvenirs and gifts can be obtained fro Kew Shop in the Orangery. Refreshments can be obtained from the Orangery Tearoom (waitress service, se menu; seasonal opening) and the Pavilion Restaurant (self-service cafeteria; open all year); both are open from 10 am to one hour before closing.

Wakehurst Place

HOW TO GET THERE Situated in West Sussex on the Turners Hill-Ardingly road (B2028) about one mile north of Ardingly, approximately 20 minutes' dri from the M23 junction of the M25.

OPENING TIMES Gardens are open every da (except Christmas Day and New Year's Day) at 10 am. Closing times vary from 4 pm in winter to 7 pm in summer.

FACILITIES Wide range of books and quali gifts can be obtained from Book Shop.

ght lunches, afternoon teas and snacks
ailable from Tea Room, open from late
arch to late October; coffee served in
ok Shop when Tea Room is closed.

HE FRIENDS OF THE
OYAL BOTANIC GARDENS, KEW

becoming a 'Friend', you will be
lping both Kew and yourself:

enefits to Kew

You will be helping to maintain the
gardens at Kew and Wakehurst Place.

You will be ensuring that vital scientific
work can go forward – the unseen but,
n the global context, most urgent task
acing Kew today. The future of the
entire plant kingdom hangs on this
work – and, through it, the health,
wealth and beauty of the environment
and all of us who live in it.

enefits to you

Unlimited free admission to Kew and
Wakehurst Place.

Exclusive Friends' magazines and
newsletters.

Privileged access to and discounts for
events at Kew.

Special Friends' tours.

Special discounts on shop purchases.

Priority access to adult education
programmes.

r more information about the Friends
d details of membership, write to:
e Manager, Friends of the Royal
tanic Gardens, Kew, Richmond, Surrey
W9 3AB.

Photo: David Palmer

Published 1990
by
Channel 4 Television
60 Charlotte Street
London W1P 2AX
and by
Royal Botanic Gardens, Kew
Richmond, Surrey TW9 3AB

© Channel 4 Television/The Board of Trustees, Royal Botanic Gardens, Kew

Produced by Broadcasting Support Services
to accompany VIEWS OF KEW
(a Granada Television production)
first shown on Channel 4 in
November – December 1990

Writer: Pat Griggs
Editor: Derek Jones
Editorial consultant: Nancy Duin
Design: Spark Ceresa
Typesetting: London Manhattan Typesetting
Printer: Haynes Cannon

Printed on environmentally friendly paper

Photographs on background front cover, back cover and inside cover: David Palmer
All other photographs courtesy of The Board of Trustees, Royal Botanic Gardens, Kew,
unless otherwise stated

Distributed by Broadcasting Support Services
and by Network Scotland,
who provide follow-up services
for viewers and listeners

For further copies,
please send a cheque/postal order for £3.00
(made payable to Channel 4 Television)
to:
VIEWS OF KEW
Box 4000
London W3 6XJ, Glasgow G12 9JQ or Cardiff CF1 9XT